GARDENING WITH
Ferns

BY REX E. MABE
ILLUSTRATION - R. GABRIEL

published by

Potpourri Press

P. O. Box 10312
Greensboro, N. C.   27404

Printed in USA

Table of Contents

Gardening With Ferns

Ferns offer a quiet, graceful beauty that is unparalleled in indoor gardens. Because of their distinct beauty, they have softened more landscapes, indoors and out, than any other type of plant. The green colors they offer are subdued, for the most part, and fit into the most classical to the most rustic setting.

Plant buyers often shy away from ferns because they are thought to be impossible to grow, with even reasonable success. This is far from being true, if a few simple practices are followed, with some regularity. One of the basic needs of ferns is humidity, and it is possible to provide enough indoors, even in small apartments. There are certainly varieties harder to grow than others, and these will be pointed out, along with those of easy culture for beginners.

Research for this book has carried me to many nurseries and through many reference books and plant encyclopedias, as well as to individuals that have enjoyed success with ferns. Through all this research, I find the basic care of ferns the same as it has always been and shall continue to be unless drastic changes are made in our indoor environment. Some of the methods I found still in use, with slight variations, are prescribed in gardening books written in the early 1900's. One thing we have now that they did not have then is constantly warm homes. These constantly warm homes eliminate most of the humidity present in the air. The grand Victorian Era was a period of beginning for terrariums and also for houseplants, including ferns. In this book we will suggest practices prescribed then, and add cultural improvements we have tested in the 1970's.

Ferns and Humidity

When thinking of ferns, think of humidity and you have the secret for growing them indoors. Most ferns require at least thirty percent humidity, but do better with forty or fifty percent. It is not often we have this much humidity in our homes in winter months, or even in the summer if we have air conditioning. To combat the dry air, some home-owners add humidifiers to the heating plant. You will seldom find this true in apartments, but there are self contained humidifiers on the market that plug into a regular electrical outlet. These humidifiers can benefit your health, as well as make it possible for ferns and other houseplants to do much better indoors.

One way to add humidity around your plants is to use saucers, or trays, half-filled with small gravel. Keep water at a level just below the gravel line so that the plant is not standing in water. The trays or saucers should be cleaned and scalded every two or three months so they will not become an area for fungus or other diseases to develop. Add some charcoal chips to the gravel to help keep the water cleaner and odorless. The gravel method can also be used to keep a fern in a decorative cachepot that does not have a facility for drainage. Leave your plant in its clay or plastic pot; add about an inch of gravel to the bottom of the cache-pot; and then set your plant in the decorative container. Be careful not to let the plant stand in water in the gravel. You can also use sphagnum moss stuffed around the pot to add humidity in decorative cachepots without drainage.

Another way of adding humidity, when the heating system is operating at its peak to keep your home warm, is to mist your plants daily. This is when the air is the dryest. Mist often in the summer also when the weather is hot and dry. Do the misting in the morning and never after mid-day. This gives your plants the opportunity to have dry foliage when the main light source is gone. Mist all ferns with broad-leaved foliage, but do not mist the fluffy ferns or other ferns with fine foliage.

You can also add humidity around the plant by wetting the container, if it is porous. I often use a pail of water for this, and simply sit the pot in the pail and allow the plant to be watered and the pot to be completely saturated. Five minutes is usually long enough, with the exception of very large pots. Take precautions not to immerse the foliage for longer than a few minutes.

Use ferns in rooms that are not heated above 72 degrees and away from drafts. They really do better in a cool, 60 degree room, and it would be advisable to place them in a cooler area at night when the home is usually kept warmer.

Watering

Watering schedules for ferns will depend upon the temperature and light where they are being used, as well as the potting soil. Check the plants daily for moisture content, but only a few varieties will need water every day. Read carefully the directions on misting under each plant, and also under the Ferns and Humidity heading. This is a part of the watering program.

If possible, use rain water for ferns. The old rain barrel is not as popular as it used to be, but it is still a good idea. Considering the fact that most folks don't have rain water readily available, the alternative is to draw water and let it sit overnight to allow chemicals to evaporate or settle. This will also allow the water to reach room temperature, which is advisable for any houseplant. If you find any plant totally dry, water it twice at half-hour intervals. The first watering will usually run right through the soil mixture, leaving only a little moisture behind, but the second watering will be better received.

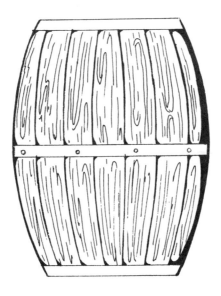

In addition to a regular watering program, one should include a schedule for cleaning plants. Do this with a mixture of one tablespoon of mild dishwashing detergent in a pint of warm water. Use a sponge and with the wider leaved ferns, wash both sides; however with finer-leaved ferns, merely mist the mixture lightly on both sides of the fronds. Do this in the morning about once a month. This will insure a clean plant, as well as assist you in pest control.

Charcoal

Many of the potting mixes in this book have charcoal listed as an ingredient and I would like to explain why. Ferns require a lot of water in the growing season, and many of them like to be kept constantly moist. For this reason we use lots of peat or sphagnum moss in the soil mixtures. The peat or sphagnum is high in acid and organic matter, and with repeated waterings can become sour. This can create gases that are harmful to the roots of plants. Charcoal absorbs these gases and acids and neutralizes the soil and water. Charcoal chips also help to insure good drainage, which is important to all ferns. Small packages of charcoal chips can be purchased at most aquarium or garden shops, but if you wish, they are easily made from cooking charcoal. The task of breaking the cooking briquets can be a chore unless they are wet. I usually get them soaking wet and put one between two bricks, step on the top brick, and presto, enough charcoal for a six inch pot.

Peat or Sphagnum Moss

Your potting mixes are greatly benefited by the use of peat or sphagnum moss, due to their moisture holding ability and the fact that they loosen the soil mix, allowing more air passage. Leaf mold is the only substitute that I know for this material, and since it is not readily available commercially, I have not used it in the recommended soil mixtures. If you do have access to leaf mold, it would be the preferred ingredient. It is of utmost importance to have any of the above materials moist when they are added to the soil mixes. If they are not moist, they will not blend with the mix, especially if you are using coarse varieties of peat moss. Mix these ingredients well so they will not be distinguishable in the soil mix. If you wish to moisten the mosses quickly, use hot water to saturate, allow it to cool, and wring out the excess. The mosses can be kept moist constantly by leaving them outside exposed to the elements. I leave mine outside in its plastic container, slit a hole in the top and add water to the package.

Pest Control

There are a number of little demons to watch for on ferns. They appear overnight sometimes, and sometimes they are on a plant when it is purchased. Always inspect a plant thoroughly before buying, and if it looks like you're getting something you are not paying for, check with your dealer. Most dealers are not aware of pests on their plants and would appreciate your informing him of his hiding guests. Do not mistake the spores on the back of fern leaflets for bugs. These spores are for reproduction, the same as seeds on other plants, and should not be taken off the plant. Your plant dealer will gladly advise you about the spores.

My pest control method is simply to carry out a constant cleaning schedule, described in the watering section of this book. The soapy solution described has proven just as satisfactory as any of the poisons on the market. If I find I have a plant heavily infested before it is brought to my attention, I spray with a house and garden insect spray and follow this with the soapy solution. In the case of brown scale on ferns, it is best to cut off fronds that are heavily infested, pick the others off with your fingers, and then bathe the plant carefully. Brown scale is a small brown insect that looks like a tiny turtle clinging to leaflets or stems of plants. This is the most-dreaded of the insects because it is the most difficult to destroy. I usually follow the method described daily until I can find no more of the little demons. You should still watch the plant closely to make sure no new babies have hatched from eggs that could have been left on the plants.

I do not advise you to use any of the strong poisons on ferns because they are not good for the plants, and I do not like poison around the house. I would much rather toss an infested plant in the garbage than risk having poisons stored in the house. If you must use poisons, be sure you have a safe place to store them, out of the reach of your children. A plant can be replaced easily, but not so with our children. Also be sure that you read carefully every word of directions offered, as well as an antidote, in case it does get into the innocent hands of children.

9

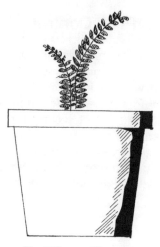

Potting Ferns

It is of utmost importance to use pots that are the right size for potting ferns. In deciding the size pot you need, the root growth is what should be taken into consideration, rather than the size of the fronds. Nothing looks more ridiculous than a tiny seedling fern in a large pot, and nothing is more discouraging to a beginning gardener than to watch a seedling fern, wondering if it will ever fill its pot. So many people think a fern needs re-potting when it is just beginning to look like a half-filled pot. Wait until your fern is literally growing out of the pot before you give it a larger home—and then increase the pot size only slightly. Aside from the fact that your fern will look better in the right size pot, there are other reasons for inspecting root systems before selecting a pot. A small plant in a large pot is difficult to water correctly, due to the fact that the excess soil holds excess moisture. The excess soil also keeps the roots of the plant from getting needed air circulation for their development.

A well-potted fern has room enough for the roots, with about an inch to grow all around the plant. Most ferns have shallow-root systems and do better in shallow pots. Learn to switch your plants from the small to the next available size, but only when it is needed. Sometimes this means re-potting several times a year, but the results are worth the trouble.

If you are using plastic pots in which to grow your ferns, make sure they have drainage holes in the bottom and on the sides of the container at the bottom. If the manufacturer has not put these holes on the sides, you can do it easily with a lighted cigarette butt. Just stick the hot end of the cigarette to the container and it will melt through easily. Do not burn holes in a pot that is housing a plant however, as this might damage the roots. Clay pots need other treatment. If you buy new ones, soak them overnight in water to allow chemicals to escape. Pot manufacturers use different types of chemicals, and the soaking treatment cleanses the pots. If you need to use the pot immediately, soak it fifteen minutes in boiling water and allow it to cool and dry before doing your potting. Used clay pots should be washed thoroughly with a strong detergent and hot water. This will remove scum or dried slimy substances which could slow down air passage through the otherwise porous surface.

To remove a fern from its pot, wet the soil thoroughly, strike the pot sharply on the side with your open hand, or against your potting table, turn the pot upside down, and the fern usually slides out very easily. If the fern does not come out readily, you can bet it needs re-potting, because the roots are clinging to the sides of the pot or growing out through the drainage holes. Sometimes I find it necessary to break a pot to get the plant out, and this is better than pulling it out because of the possible damage to the roots and top-growth.

Use an inch of broken crockery in the bottom of your clay pots that only have one drainage hole. Alternatives for the broken crockery could be gravel or broken sticks. The purpose here is to insure that the drainage holes stay open for free passage of excess water and to allow air to flow through freely. With plastic pots or other pots with several drainage holes, I use milled sphagnum moss in the bottom of the container, filled to just above the holes on the sides. I find this material is cleaner in the long run, keeping the soil from spilling out the side holes when you are watering or moving the plant.

The potting itself is simple. After you have put in the drainage material, pour in some of the recommended soil mixture. Do not pack it, but simply jar the pot and it will settle nicely. When it is full enough, place the plant in the pot with the roots spread outward to the sides of the pot. Then add enough soil to bring the level to about one inch below the top of the pot. This will be important when watering. Press the soil firmly around the roots of the plant and add more if necessary, but do not cover the crown of the plant. Water lightly and watch your fern give birth to new fronds.

Polystichum Tsus Simenese

Polystichum tsus-simenese is a dwarf member of a group of ferns often referred to as holly ferns. This one is native to Japan and China. It has emerald green fronds that supposedly reach a maximum height of two feet. I have never seen one with fronds over ten inches in length, and can't imagine it being as attractive in a large size. The fronds grow densely and form a rosette that looks great in a terrarium, a small pot, or a hanging container. A very close look at the individual leaflets reveals the slight similarity to some of the other ferns referred to as holly ferns. The broken leaflets, that look like more small fern fronds, come to a sharp point like the hollys we know. Their texture is a little stiff at maturity, but never stiff enough to prick even the daintiest finger.

Use a potting mix of equal parts of peat moss, sand, and garden or packaged potting soil. These ferns prefer a slightly acid soil mixture, so do not use lime as is recommended for many of the others. Keep the soil constantly moist from March to October. In other months water only when it has become dry. This fern likes humidity and should be used in a saucer that is half-filled with gravel and water to keep moisture nearby, especially when it is exposed to a hot, dry room. It does not like to have its foliage misted, although it should be given a warm misting every couple of months to keep the foliage clean. Be sure to do this in the morning so that the foliage will be dry before nightfall. Use in bright to low light situations or morning sun only. This type of fern is recommended for beginners as it is very tolerant and forgiving.

Holly Fern

There are a number of ferns referred to as holly ferns, and this one really deserves the name, because it does look much like its namesake. The botanical name of this plant is **cyrtomium falcatum.** It is sometimes referred to as the Japanese holly fern because it is native to Japan. The fronds will grow to three feet long under good growing conditions, but this seldom happens in a pot. They are normally mature at eighteen to thirty inches indoors. The foliage is a very dark green, leathery in texture, and very shiny like the leaves of holly. The leaflets are elongated-ovals, coming to a point, and are from one to two inches wide and three to four inches long.

The holly fern is used outdoors in mild climates and is making progress as a houseplant. Its chief enemy indoors is heat. Display it on a cool sun porch or other area that never gets above seventy-five degrees, and it will do well. Give it low to medium light. Keep the soil moist from April to September and water when dry in other months. For outdoor use, it should be used in shade only and protected from temperatures below forty degrees. The soil mixture should include one-third soil, one-third peat moss, and one third coarse sand and small gravel mixed in equal parts. Add a cup of charcoal chips and a cup of dried cow manure to a gallon of this mix. I would call this a plant for collectors of ferns, although it is of easy culture.

Bird's Nest Fern

This fern is one of my favorites and was used previously in another of my books, "Gardening With Houseplants." I cannot, however, let an opportunity pass to recommend the bird's nest fern, which is named botanically **asplenium nidus.** It is indeed an unusual member of the fern family, due to its slightly ruffled undivided fronds. The fronds are bright green and grow to a maximum of three feet in length, although by keeping them pot bound, they will maintain a smaller size. I placed two small plants in four inch pots on the mantel in a friend's home a year ago, and they continue to grow nicely, producing fronds about seven inches in length. To grow a large plant it is necessary to re-pot twice annually, preferably in April and again in August, increasing the pot size about an inch each time. Personally, I prefer the plant in its smaller sizes, because of its added usefulness in decorative cachepots on small tables, etageres and mantels.

The potting mix should contain one-third potting soil, one-third peat moss, and one-third sand, small gravel, and charcoal chips mixed in equal parts. It should be fed every three months with one of the water soluble plant foods. It does well in low to bright light and should never be used in direct sun. Keep it constantly moist, and give it occasional mistings and a monthly bath.

Button Fern

This is an appealing little fern that is of easy culture and is recommended for beginning fern growers. The botanical name for the button fern is **pellaea rotundifolia.** It is native to New Zealand, where it lives near limestone cliffs and has another common name, cliff brake. This fern has small round leaflets that grow on tiny brownish stems. The leaflets are dark and shiny green, developing a slight mahogany cast to them as they grow. They are small at maturity, with fronds seldom getting longer than twelve inches, which makes them excellent plants for small hanging baskets or terrariums. I find them interesting to watch, particularly in the growing season. Sometimes they will have a dozen new fronds unfolding at the same time, and they will be in all the development stages.

Water this fern when the soil becomes dry to the touch. Water it thoroughly at that time and not before, or you will find the fern disappointing. Mist it occasionally, and bathe it once a month with the recommended soap and water solution. In the winter it should be used where it will get bright light, but in the summer, it would be at home in any part of your house, where there is subdued light. Use a potting mix of one-third garden or packaged potting soil, one-third peat moss, with the other third including equal parts sand, charcoal, and coarse sand. Add one heaping teaspoon of lime to a quart of this potting mix.

Pellea Viridis

There are two different varieties of **pellea viridis,** one is called **viridis,** and the other, with a slight variation in leaf structure, is called, **viridis macrophylla.** They are of the same family as the button fern, **pellaea rotundifolia,** and require the same soil mixture. These two varieties like to be kept constantly moist, which is the only difference between the culture of the **viridis** and **rotundifolia.** The **viridis** varieties are native to Africa. Both have dark green, leather foliage on dark brown, wiry stems. Their growth habit is somewhat bushy, making it most useful as a pot plant. The fronds are from one to two and one-half feet in length. The **viridis** variety has somewhat larger leaflets on the fronds than does the **macrophylla.** They are both handsome plants that are of easy culture and are recommended for beginners.

Use them always in containers with a facility for drainage. They look especially good in a room with dark paneling, if there is a north or east window for good light. A monthly bath and an occasional misting are beneficial.

Asparagus Ferns

The asparagus ferns are not really ferns at all, but they have been referred to as such for years. They are members of the **liliaceae** family and have tiny blossoms and reproduce by seeds rather than by spores. They can also be propagated by dividing the plants in the spring. All the ornamental asparagus ferns are native to Africa, and have fleshy roots that are similar to tiny potatoes. These roots are capable of sustaining the plant for days without any added moisture.

The foliage of all these plants is fine and feathery in texture. The **plumosus** variety is the finest textured and has dark green coloring. The most popular variety, **sprengeri,** has light green fronds that flow generously from its container. **Meyeri** is still another soft green color with spikey stems densely covered with fine foliage. **Myriocladus** has dark green foliage that resembles tiny pine needles. It grows on stems from ten to eighteen inches that look like miniature trees when viewed individually.

Give the asparagus ferns bright light and rich soil and they make beautiful houseplants. The potting mix should include one-third garden or packaged potting soil, one-third peat moss, and one-third sand. To a gallon of this mixture, add one pint of dried cow manure. From April to September, keep the plants constantly moist and feed weekly with a water-soluble plant food diluted to half-strength. In other months, water the plant only when it is dry, and feed monthly. The asparagus ferns like lots of light and can take direct sun year-round, but should be protected from the hot sun of mid-day in summer. They will also do well in places that are very light, without direct sun.

I have found these ferns useful in pots when they are small, and when larger, in hanging containers near or in front of sunny windows.

Pteris Ferns

The several popular varieties of **pteris** are often referred to as brake ferns. There are many variations of leaf structure and size in this fern family, which is native to many different areas of the globe. They all seem to have one thing in common—the growth of the plant above the soil line seems to have a thin line between it and the plant's root system. This sometimes causes the plants to lean to the side of the container in which it is planted. It might be necessary at times to add more soil around the crown of the plant and firm it lightly to keep the fern steady in its pot. Do not, however, cover the crown of the plant, which should be totally exposed just above the soil line.

The **pteris** ferns all have the same cultural and soil requirements. Give them bright light in months from September to March; water only when the plant has become dry; and do not feed. In other months, keep them constantly moist and feed them monthly with a plant food such as fish emulsion. Keep them out of direct sun rays and mist often all year round. A good potting mix should include one-third garden or packaged potting soil, one-third peat moss, with sand, small gravel and charcoal chips, mixed in equal parts, making up the other one-third of the mixture. The **pteris** ferns are of easy culture and recommended for beginners.

Pteris Cretica

This is another fern family that has proven its worth and many variations are appearing on the market with names varying in different locales. The family is **pteris cretica,** and the variations will be listed as they are known in the Southeast. Any difficulty in name identification in other areas should be solved by comparing the illustrations and being satisfied that the name used in your area is also correct.

The most popular of the **pteris cretica** family is a variety known as **wimsetti,** followed closely in popularity by **rivertoniana.** Another popular variety is **albolineata** which has long slender leaflets and is known as ribbon brake. This variety is variegated, with silvery-white bands down the center of the leaflets. It is also available in solid green. The varieties of **pteris** ferns have stiff slender stems that grow upright and hold their foliage aloft. Foliage does not cover the lower portion of the stem. As the pot fills with new fronds, they will eventually form a drooping habit. These ferns are recommended for pot plants only.

Pteris Tremula

This is the largest growing member of the **pteris** family. The fronds grow upright to three feet on a mature plant, but seldom does this happen in a home garden. They usually reach about two feet in height. The fronds are up to twelve inches wide at the base, and taper to a point. The stems are wiry and stiff in appearance, but as the fronds mature they hang gracefully to the side of the pot, giving it an open, airy appearance. The fronds are light yellow-green in early stages, but get darker with maturity. The **tremula** is native to Australia and New Zealand.

Tremula is a vigorous grower from its baby stages, and usually produces fronds of maximum height in its first year of growth. I find the plant useful at all stages. When it is small, it works well on side tables or etageres. Later it can be placed on fern stands, and at maturity, on the floor. The defined fronds make beautiful patterns when used with indirect lighting, indoors or out. I often substitute the mature **tremulas** for a small palm in doing plant displays for porches.

Maidenhair Fern

This is said by many people to be the most beautiful fern grown—and by some to be the most difficult. The botanical name of the most popular of its many varieties, is **adiantum cuneatum.** It has fronds that range from eight to fifteen inches long and four to eight inches wide. These fronds are held on tiny, wiry stems, and have leaflets that are ever so delicate and lacy. The color is dark green at maturity and very light green as the fronds first unfurl. One nurseryman told me that a healthy maidenhair plant would have fronds at all stages of development—some that are light green, others dark green, and even others that are dying. These dying fronds will turn brown and should be carefully cut away. This pruning will make your plant look better as well as encourage new growth.

The maidenhair has a definite resting period in the winter, usually from November to March, and during that time should be watered less than in the growing season, which is the rest of the year. If you water too much in the winter months, the plant will go into a complete slump, but by taking away dead fronds and watering lightly, it will come back with renewed vigor in March. When the dormancy period is over, the plant will start to grow lots of new fronds and fill a small pot in a couple of months.

The **cuneatum** is native to tropical Brazil, which accounts for the fact that it needs humidity and moist soil conditions. There are many different methods of watering that work for different people. I prefer to keep mine steadily moist, but not soggy, in the growing season. Soggy soil will cut off the root's air supply and cause the roots to rot. In the months when the fern is not making new growth, it should be kept only slightly moist. The maidenhair likes light, but not direct sun. Don't use the plant in a dark area, or you will have spindly growth that will usually collapse before it reaches maturity. Direct sun will cause the newest fronds to turn brown before they have a chance to turn a dark green.

Do not mist the maidenhair fern—unless you are giving it a bath—and do this lightly, and in the morning. Provide as much air as possible, avoiding drafts, and keep in a cool place. It does not like temperatures above seventy degrees or below forty-five degrees. The potting mix should include one-half peat moss, one-fourth soil, and a mixture of sand, charcoal chips and dried cow manure, mixed in equal parts, for the other one-fourth. To a gallon of this mixture add one-half cup of ground limestone.

Pink Maidenhair

Pink maidenhair gets its name from the scant pink coloring on new fronds. This variety is known botanically as **adiantum hispidulum** and has the same cultural require-ments as the **cuneatum.** The delicate look again prevails as with the **cuneatum,** but the frond shape is quite different. The stems are small and wiry, usually about eight to twelve inches long. On the end of the stem a beautiful, five-spiked, fanshaped frond is formed. These five spikes are leaflets that have leaflets along their very fine stems, and often the side spikes will have a smaller spike at the base.

The center spike is the longest with the two side spikes smaller, to make the fan shape. The overall frond is from five to nine inches wide at the point where the foliage begins. The stem is generally about twelve inches long. This gives the fronds a graceful look, with the foliage being held aloft by tiny black, almost invisible stems.

Pacific Maid

This fern has created quite a rage for lovers of the maidenhair ferns. It has the most beautiful lush foliage one can imagine, that literally curls and ruffles as it grows. This variety of maidenhair is known botanically as **adiantum tenerum wrightii,** and commonly as Pacific maid. The foliage looks much like the **cuneatum,** but the leaflets are larger and a bit more ruffled around the edges. The coloring is dark green at maturity, with lighter green on new fronds. The combination of the two colors give the plant its greatest appeal. The Pacific maid has the same cultural requirements as the **cuneatum** and the **hispidulum.**

I was surprised to learn that the Pacific maid variety of maidenhair is not readily available across the country, but I am sure it will be in the next couple of years. I feel most fortunate to know nurserymen here in the Southeast that grow these ferns from spores and market them commercially. Spores are the dustlike particles that form on the back of a mature fern's leaflets. A few years ago I had a bad experience when I ordered some of these spores. When I received them, and opened the packet, I found no seeds at all. Whereupon, I wrote the seedsman and he sent me another packet in which, again, I found no seeds. Becoming a little upset, I called the company to complain. They asked me to check my packets again and explained how tiny the spores, not seeds, were. The spores were there, to my embarrassment, but after marigold and zinnia seeds, they appeared the size of the tiniest speck of dust. Being a complete novice, I had no luck with the spores and it was much later before I acquired one of the beautiful Pacific maid ferns.

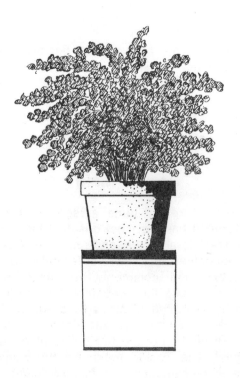

I have learned that the easy way to get new plants is to simply divide the plant by separating the roots carefully and placing new seedlings into individual pots for development.

The above illustration shows spore cases, called **sori,** on the back of a mature pacific maid fern frond. Each of these cases hold many spores and one leaflet would yield enough to start a small fern crop. When the spore cases get brownish in color, place a frond or leaflet, depending on how many spores you want, in an envelope and put it in a dry warm place for a couple of days. The spore cases will open during this time and release spores that you can sow to increase your fern supply. Growing ferns from spores is possible in the home, but they must be sown in containers that have been sterilized and can maintain high humidity. One such container would be a terrarium bowl or aquarium tank. The spores should be placed on the top of the soil mix rather than buried, as I had tried to do in my original effort. The soil mixture could be placed in the bottom of a terrarium container or in a pot and placed in an aquarium tank in individual pots, if you are trying to grow different kinds of ferns. The potting mix should include, one-fourth coarse sand, one-fourth small gravel, one-fourth garden soil, and one-fourth milled sphagnum moss. All these ingredients, including the pots, which should be clay, will need to be sterilized. This can be done by baking them in a 250 degree oven for one hour. Mix the sand, soil and small gravel together, but keep the sphagnum moss separate. Place the sphagnum moss in the bottom of your container, making a bed for your other mixture. Now place the sand, soil and gravel mixture over the sphagnum and level it off by jarring the pot. Dampen the pot and the soil mix by soaking them in a container of water in which the water level is just below the pot's rim. Now you are ready to sow spores. The sowing of the spores is difficult, especially in getting even distribution over the potting mix. This can be made a little simpler by placing the spores on a whtie sheet of paper and distributing them by shaking the paper. If the sowing process is done by dropping them from the hand, it would be hard to tell when they were dropped since they are so small. The white paper allows you to see what you are sowing and will aid in a more even distribution.

After you have done the sowing, place the container under glass and keep it constantly moist. If the potting mix should dry out only once, your success is very improbable. Watch the container daily for moisture content. If a lot of condensation forms on the side or top of the glass container, remove some of it by wiping it with a clean paper towel. There should be light condensation at all times, which is in the form of very small droplets. If there are large droplets, there is too much condensation. If you need to add moisture—do it with a mister. The spores should produce signs of new plants in from five days to nine months, depending on the variety.

Rabbit's Foot Fern

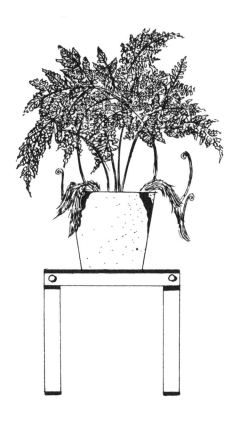

This is a peculiar fern because of its rhizomes that are on the surface of the soil and crawl down the side of its container. These rhizomes are gray-white, hair-like growth which looks much like a rabbit's foot. It is a member of the **davallia** fern family which is a member of the family, **polypodiaceae.** The rabbit's foot fern is known botanically as **davallia fejeensis.** Its fronds are borne directly out of the hairy rhizomes and are held on stiff stems that are from twelve to eighteen inches tall. The foliage is fine and lacy on the top half of the stem. The foliage color is soft green at early stages, turning darker green at maturity.

There are several other members of the **davallia** family that are interesting to grow. One is the **bullata** which is called the squirrel's foot fern, due to it's brown, creeping rhizomes. **Davallia griffithiana** is another, and is much like the **fejeensis** in growth habit and texture. The **solida** is a larger fern with bright green fronds that are held aloft by stiff stems.

Due to the peculiar habit of these plants' rhizomes, they require a slightly different type of potting. The soil mix should be poured into the pot or basket with the rhizomes placed on top of it and anchored with a wire or string until a plant is well established.

The **davallias** are native to tropical areas where they get lots of humidity and have moist soil conditions. Your success in growing the plants will depend on how well you can duplicate those conditions. A wooden or wire hanging basket makes an interesting container for these ferns. Not only will you get to enjoy the foliage, you will enjoy watching the rabbit's feet creep down the sides and bear new fronds off the side of the container. The soil mixture for these plants should include one-fourth garden or packaged potting soil, one-fourth peat moss, one-fourth finely chopped pine-bark mulch or some textured equivalent, and one-fourth small gravel and sand mixed in equal parts. Add one pint of charcoal chips to a gallon of this mixture. Feed these ferns monthly from March to September with a natural plant food such as fish emulsion. Although some of these varieties have fine, lacy foliage, they do like misting and lots of it, especially when used in dry conditions. While most lacy or fluffy ferns cannot tolerate misting, these thrive on it, due to their open growth which allows free air passage in and around the fronds. Give them good light year round; some morning sun is beneficial in winter, but otherwise they should be used in a shady area.

Hare's Foot Fern

The question that immediately comes to mind here is, isn't a hare and a rabbit the same thing? The answer is "yes," but there is a difference in size. A hare has longer ears, larger hind legs, and bigger feet. The same is true with the hare's foot fern. It has larger rhizomes, longer stems, and the foliage is larger. The cultural requirements and potting mix prescribed for rabbit's foot would also apply to the hare's foot fern.

The hare's foot is sometimes called the blue-leaved hare's foot, due to its bluish-green foliage which somewhat resembles a split-leaf philodendron. The botanical name of this fern is **polypodium aureum mandaianum,** which means the fern is of the same original family as the rabbit's foot—**polypodiceae.**

The rhizomes of the hare's foot fern are a brown color and are generally about the size of a man's thumb. The stems range from eighteen to thirty inches tall, and the foliage is from eight to fifteen inches long, with deep-scalloped edges. The foliage of the fern generally bows while the stems are upright in growth habit. This plant requires a large space when it is mature, and is considered an easy plant to grow. I would not recommend it to beginners, but it is certainly worth a try when you are experienced with plants.

Staghorn Fern

This is probably the most unusual member of the fern family, and never fails to draw lots of attention. It produces two different types of fronds, and is strictly an epiphyte (meaning it grows on the trunks or in crevices of trees). It is known botanically as **platycerium bifurcatum** and commonly as the staghorn fern. The common name is derived from one type of the fern's fronds, which indeed resemble a stag's horns. The other type of frond is round and flat and grows directly against its mount, whether it be a tree in a tropical forest in Africa or on a slab in your garden room. The round, flat frond bears no spores (seed), but collects moisture and food for the long horn-shaped fronds. This is a very slow-growing fern and one would not have to worry about its ever over-taking its limits. The baby fronds are four to six inches long, but reach lengths of three and four feet, after years of growth. The fronds are gray-green in color and are deeply divided. They are narrow at the base and spread to eighteen inch widths at the tips. The round, flat frond varies from 4 to 12 inches in diameter.

The plant requires good humidity and in the summer should be watered every day, especially if it is used outside. In the winter, it can be watered less often, but daily misting should be kept up year round.

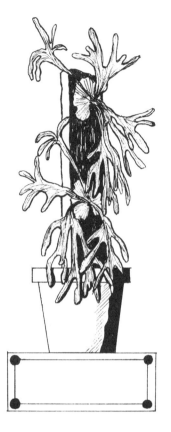

The staghorn fern should be mounted to a cedar, red-wood, or cork slab. This is done by placing the flat frond against the slab and securing it with a wire or a string. Behind the flat frond, place a mixture of peat moss, half-decayed oak leaves, and finely chopped sphagnum moss mixed in equal parts. Add a few charcoal chips to prevent the mix from becoming sour, and you are ready to grow a real conversation piece. The roots of the staghorn are behind the flat frond and will eventually support the plant. Then the wire or string can be removed.

The plant is of easy culture if the misting and watering program is followed. It does not require any plant food, but a yearly top-dressing of the above soil mixture should be added. Use the plant on a slab fastened to a patio or garden room wall, or on a slab that is anchored in a pot. Give it bright light, but avoid using it in direct sun.

The Boston Fern Family

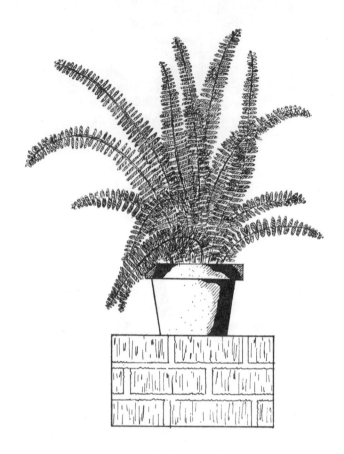

Sword Fern

The sword fern was once the most popular fern in use for indoor gardens. It was the first fern to be used as a major plant for the trade. The plant is still in use and preferred by some people, but its many variations are more popular today. The sword fern is the first member of a large family of ferns known botanically as **nephrolepis exalta,** the most popular of which is the Boston fern. There are definite resemblances between the two, and the sword fern is often called a wild Boston. It is native from Florida to Brazil, also in Asia and Africa.

The fronds of the sword fern are from two to five feet long and two to five inches wide. The leaflets are flat, singular and a dark green. The fronds grow upright and arch as they develop in length, making it a showy pot plant. This fern can take more sun than other members of the family. It should be used in partial shade in summer, and in an area where it will get a couple of hours of sun every day during the winter. The watering schedule in summer is the same as the other Boston ferns, but it does not use as much water—so be careful not to overwater, especially in winter. The sword fern is one of the easiest to grow, and is recommended most heartily for beginning indoor gardeners.

Boston Fern

The botanical name of the Boston fern is **nephrolepis exalta bostoniensis.** It is a direct descendant of the sword fern and was first discovered in the early 1890's. The fern was discovered in Boston where it was being sold under another name, hence the name **bostoniensis.** The Boston fern just happened; it was not due to any nurserymen doing any tricks with the spores and hybridizing, as is often thought. One grower said it came about due to a change in genes, and that makes more sense than some of the other yarns I have heard. So for our own use, let's just assume it is another of mother nature's beautiful gifts.

The **nephrolepis exalta bostoniensis** is now very much in demand, and has been ever since its discovery because of the graceful fronds it produces. They range from twelve inches to four feet long and three to six inches wide, depending on the different variations of this fern. The original **bostoniensis** had fronds about two feet in length, and the leaflets were flat and a little wider than the sword fern. The upright growth was seldom over eight inches, as they droop in early stages. This growth habit brought about the development and manufacture of the fern stand. They are most often used on stands and in baskets because of their drooping habit.

Some of the ferns we know as Boston today have more upright growth and the leaflets are slightly cupped at the ends, giving them a frilled effect. This fern is called Boston compacta, due to its very compact growth habit. It is a beautiful pot or basket plant. At maturity the plant gets so full of growth, that one wonders how it can possibly keep producing fronds. The fronds are from two to three feet in length and about three inches wide, with the same soft green color as the Boston exalta. Incidentally, the botanical name of the Boston compacta would be **nephrolepis exalta bostoniensis compacta.** For that reason, and because of the following ferns listed under this heading, we will drop the use of botanical names. They get more complicated with the addition of each variation, and they are commonly known by fluffy ruffle, whitmanii, or shadow lace. More than likely if you went to purchase a fern such as Boston compacta and asked for it by the four word name listed above, you would be peered at severely and asked to repeat what you had said.

At this point it will be necessary to describe some of the ways that ferns are identified botanically according to their leaf structure, as you will see in some of the next ferns appearing in the book.

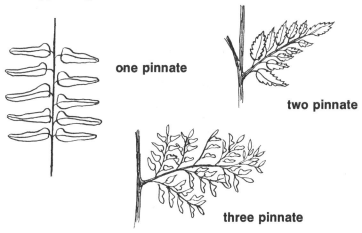

one pinnate

two pinnate

three pinnate

To begin this leaf definition, let's first look at one frond, which is one stem or branch coming from the base of the plant. This frond has leaflets on each side, from near the base of the stem, normally ending in a point. These leaflets are referred to in botanical terms as **pinnate.** (A single leaflet is called **pinna**). A fern that is described as being pinnate, has single leaflets or single pinna. A sword fern is one pinnate; a fluffy ruffle is two—which means the leaflet is split by single growths on each side. Some of the other forms of fluffy ruffle are called doubles and are three pinnate, meaning the leaflets have leaflets that are divided. These three pinnate leaflets look like a frond itself, in very miniature sizes. This goes on and on. There is a four, five and six pinnate leaflet. The verona variety of the whitmanii fern will often have leaflets that are all mixed together, from one pinnate to six pinnate. This is often true in the Boston fern family. Some of the fronds will revert back to the growth of each of the plants of its heredity. These are the only botanical explanations of ferns I will attempt to pass along. I think they will be helpful to you in understanding some of the written matter about ferns, and will certainly help me in getting across descriptions of the rest of the Boston fern family.

Whitmanii

The whitmanii fern has several variations, but they are all lacy-looking in overall appearance. The first variety of whitmanii is three pinnate, with fronds ranging from eighteen to twenty-four inches in length and four to seven inches wide. This variety is the easiest of the fluffy ferns to care for. The whitmanii is generally fast-growing, and makes a beautiful pot or hanging basket in a single year of growth. This variety will usually keep the same foliage throughout, but will revert occasionally to the Boston fern fronds. Some people will advise you to take out the fronds that revert to the Boston type, but unless you plan to propagate or prefer it with all lacy fronds, it is all right to leave the odd fronds. I don't usually take the reverted fronds out, because I like to see the different fronds together on a single plant. It holds special interest because you can see part of the fern's family tree together on one plant.

Whitmanii Verona

Verona is indeed a beauty and would be the next easiest of the fluffy ferns to grow. Its fronds are very light and airy, with three, four, five and six pinnate leaflets. The stems are thin and wiry, giving the entire plant a delicate appearance. The plant is sometimes referred to as shadow lace, but the shadow lace is still different. Verona has light, lettuce-green foliage, and the fronds normally cascade when they are half-way to maturity. Due to the short lengths of the fronds, this makes a beautiful pot plant. A pot that is six inches in height will keep the foliage from the table on which it is placed. The fronds range from twelve to eighteen inches in length and are about four inches wide. This plant does not like misting directly on the foliage. I usually mist around the plant and moisten the pot when I want to add humidity.

Fluffy Ruffle

There are several fluffy ruffle ferns that make beautiful basket or fern stand plants. They have long fronds, to three feet, and need more height than you normally find in a pot for indoor use. The single fluffy ruffle is three pinnate; the double fluffy ruffle is four or five pinnate; and the super-double fluffy ruffle is five or six pinnate. Of these the single fluffy is the easiest to keep in healthy condition. The double and super-double are heavier in texture, and I find them difficult to grow. They all like humidity, and lots of it, but they, like the verona, do not like to have their foliage misted. These are all beautiful ferns, but wait until some of the simpler ones have been mastered before trying them, especially the double and super-double.

One of the ruffle ferns that goes by the name of Florida ruffle is a more easily cultivated member of this family. I haven't been able to locate a botanical name for it, although I have found that it is definitely of the Boston family. Commercial growers market it as Florida ruffle and are satisfied with that name only. The leaflets are four and five pinnate, and the fronds are eighteen to twenty-four inches in length and three to five inches wide. The ones I have grown are not as demanding of humidity as the other ruffle ferns. The fronds are upright to a semi-droop, due to very stiff stems. It has dark green coloring and lots of fluffy foliage. It makes a beautiful pot plant when it is small, and later can be a nice plant for a hanging basket or fern stand. This one prefers not to be misted directly on its foliage.

Petticoat Fern

This is another member of the Boston fern family, **nephrolepis exalta.** There is no botanical name available for the fern at present but I am sure there will be, because petticoat is much too simple a name for this outstanding plant. The first time I saw the plant, I was absolutely awe struck by its distinct beauty. There are three varieties of the petticoat described here, with drawings to help in identification. The chief grower of these ferns in the southeast identifies one as the Boston petticoat and another as the sword petticoat. The third variety was obtained from another grower, and he had no special name for his model, so I'll call it whitmanii petticoat, because the fronds resemble the whitmanii varieties of the Boston fern.

The Boston petticoat has soft green foliage that is frilly on the tips of the leaflets. The fronds are from two to four feet long, with four to six inch fronds extending from the ends or tips of the stems. This tip growth spreads and forks to make a fluffy mass of foliage that represents the crinoline at the bottom of an old fashioned petticoat. It grows very full at maturity, with long fronds arching out from the base of the plant, and with lots of new growth going upright until they develop their crinoline that gracefully arches them downward. All three varieties have this same growth habit, with slight differences.

The sword petticoat, named for the sword fern, has flat, dark green leaflets on fronds that are of the same length as the Boston petticoat. The dark green color of this variety makes it a more striking plant, but it does not develop as thick a growth habit as does the Boston.

The whitmanii petticoat does not develop the tip crinoline on every frond, but it does develop split leaflets on the sides of the stem. The overall growth habit is somewhat larger in circumference, since all the fronds do not droop from the weight of the crinoline. This plant has a lacy look, but it is not as lacy as some of the whitmanii varieties. This variety is grass green in color, with practically all fronds reaching three to four feet in length. The culture of these varieties is the same as the other Boston ferns.

Boston Fern Culture

The care of all of these members of the Boston fern family is essentially the same. There are a few variations that will be outlined here. The main difference is that which I have noted already in the descriptions of the fluffy and whitmanii varieties—that is, the misting. Do not mist the fluffy and whitmanii varieties directly. Mist around the plant and dampen the container to add humidity. Misting of the other varieties, which have one pinnate leaflets, is beneficial. The reason for not misting the finer leaved varieties is that the dense foliage sometimes has difficulty drying out. Excessive moisture on their foliage will cause the leaflets to turn brown and eventually fall apart.

A recommended potting mixture for the Boston fern family should include one-third garden or packaged potting soil, one-third sand or perlite, and one-third peat or shredded sphagnum moss. Add to a gallon of this mixture one pint dried cow manure, one-half pint crushed charcoal, and a half-pint of small gravel. They like steadily moist soil. Do not let them get bone dry, and do not keep them soggy. Give them a couple of hours of weak sun in the winter, either early morning or late afternoon, and keep them in the shade in other seasons. A monthly feeding of a natural plant food, such as fish emulsion, should be applied from April to September, and in other months, feed every other month or continue to feed monthly with your plant food diluted to half-strength. Most ferns do not mind being pot-bound and the Boston is no exception.

Hardy Ferns

A growing number of hardy ferns are becoming available for planting in outdoor gardens. This is indeed great news for gardeners because ferns are easy to grow outside if you can supply them with moist shady conditions. The hardy varieties greet you with new growth every spring, usually just after the tulips have started to grow. In referring to different types of ferns for outdoor gardens, it would be best to check those that grow in the woodlands in your locale. The common woods ferns are not common at all when they are growing in your private garden and those would be the ones to try first. After you have succeeded with them, then branch out and add to your collection by ordering plants from catalogs listing hardy ferns.

I have found in moving ferns from the woodlands that it is almost an effortless way to get new plants for my garden and they always seem to come out being my favorites. I like to dig them in early spring after a rainy spell. I get the plant with its entire root system and some extra half-rotted leaves, bring it home and plant it that day. The hole where you are to plant the fern should be about twice the size of the roots you have collected. Loosen the soil in the bottom of this hole as well as the soil around it. Now place some of the loose soil back into the hole, so that when you place your fern it will be just below the existing soil level. Then put the extra half-rotted leaves around the base of the plant and fill the hole with the rest of the loose soil taken from the hole. Do not cover the fronds or the crown of the plant. The next day the fern should be watered generously in the morning. If there is need for more soil, add more half-rotted leaves instead. This will mulch the fern to give it extra moisture as well as feed the plant and keep unwanted weeds from growing. Try not to disturb the plant any further. If there is a long dry spell, it would be well to water it occasionally, but when you do water, water thoroughly, do not just sprinkle water around the plant.

In the spring the plant will produce many fronds and make a nice trouble-free plant that blends into any garden. By summer, it should be full grown and add a refreshing coolness to your outdoor garden. In the fall the fronds will start to die, after Jack Frost makes his first cool visit. Do not remove the dead fronds. Allow them to stay there until the following spring when they will hide themselves with new fronds. The dead fern fronds give the plant protection through the winter and protects the crown of the plant. In areas where winter temperatures get below freezing often, it would be a good idea to add some extra leaves for mulch and extra protection from freezing and thawing temperatures. The bulk of the mulch can be removed in the spring.

The hardy ferns that I have tried or have seen fellow gardeners try with great success here in North Carolina are many and varied. One of the prettiest, and probably the most sought-after is the Northern maidenhair, which is known botanically as **adiantum pedatum.** It looks much like the pink maidenhair, listed elsewhere in this book. The major exception in looks is the spiked-leaflets. The pink maidenhair has five major spiked leaflets with two small secondary ones and the Northern maidenhair has eight major and two secondary. It is light green in color and grows from one to two feet in height. One of my favorites of the hardy ferns is the **ebony spleenwort** which grows to different sizes in different places. In and around rocks or on cliffsides it will grow fronds from four to six inches long but in deep humusy soil it will grow them to eighteen inches. The fronds are very slender, seldom over two inches wide, and look like a minature Boston fern. I use these ferns in terrariums, among rocks in the garden, beside walks or any other moist shady place where there is a few inches of planting space. This fern will tolerate partial sun if the soil is kept moist. The common woods fern in most areas here in the Southeast is the **polypody** which looks again like the Boston fern with fronds from ten to 24 inches long. In moist, deep woods in this area, one can see a carpet of these beautiful ferns from May to October. I find these very tolerant for garden use.

I have several cinnamon ferns growing in deep shade around our home that seem to grow prettier every day. They have three-foot long fronds that fall gracefully to the sides and others that maintain an upright growth habit. The stem turns a cinnamon color as the fronds mature and the spores are borne on fronds that first appear green, but instead of unfurling, they turn cinnamon and make a beautiful stiff

45

spike with clusters of spore cases that are often dried and used in winter bouquets. This fern can also be grown in areas with partial sun. The resurrection fern is another interesting little fern that's fun to have around. It usually grows on stumps or fallen trees in damp areas but can be used in rock gardens or crevices that one might enjoy having some greenery. It has short fronds, about seven inches at maximum, and grows on a vine. It looks, again, much like a miniature Boston fern. In wet weather you will find the short little fronds unfurled looking very much alive but a drought will make it turn brown and curl-up for protection. When watered it quickly comes alive again like magic. Other hardy ferns that will do well are the Christmas fern, lady fern, Virginia chain fern, sensitive fern, royal fern, and the rattlesnake fern.

Before you go to the woods to start digging ferns for your garden, make sure you have permission from the land owner. Then, take only the ferns you can use. After you have dug a fern, re-fill the hole from which you have taken it with soil or dead leaves. If the hole is left open it will cause soil erosion. Do not take ferns that are growing on banks or in other areas where they are important in the prevention of soil erosion. I try to get mine in a flat area, or where there are lots of rock. One place you can usually get permission to dig ferns is where new construction is going to take place. Unfortunately they usually have to remove most of the trees and undergrowth.

SOLID BRASS PLANT MISTER
(guaranteed to tarnish)

for

cleaning plants and providing
moisture and humidity

If you are unable to find this attractive brass plant mister locally, we will be happy to send one to you.

Potpourri Press
P. O. Box 10312
Greensboro, N. C. 27404

Gentlemen:

Please send me _____ plant misters at $4.00 each, postage paid.

Name_____

Street_____

City_____ Zip_____

Rex Mabe describes himself as "a garden club lecturer, wine drinker and a posey smeller" with wide experience in growing and loving plants. In addition to formal training, he acquired six years of practical experience while working for a florist. In 1971, Rex opened "The Arbor House", a shop in an old home in Greensboro, North Carolina. There he sells plants of all types, plants and sells terrariums, answers millions of questions about why "my Aunt Julia's ferns are healthy and beautiful and mine just wither and die", and, incidentally — resides.

"I love plants and plants love me, and that's life for me . . . I have visited and talked with little old ladies all over, as well as many experienced nurserymen, to gain insight into plant problems and how to solve them . . . I worked in nurseries for free while in the Navy and ended up with house-plants all over the barracks—and was pointed at a lot! . . . Raising tobacco was my father's livelihood. I was raised in the woodland and sometimes wish I was back . . ."

Other gardening books from Potpourri Press include:
GARDENING WITH FLOWERING HOUSEPLANTS
GARDENING IN HANGING BASKETS
GARDENING WITH HERBS
GARDENING WITH HOUSEPLANTS
GARDENING WITH TERRARIUMS

A complete list of other Potpourri Press publications available upon request.
(Shipped in a plain brown wrapper.)